HOW-TO LIBRARY

DECORATING EGGS

By Dana Meachen Rau • Illustrated by Kathleen Petelinsek

CHERRY LAKE PUBLISHING • ANN ARBOR, MICHIGAN

CHERRY LAKE Publishing

Published in the United States of America by Cherry Lake Publishing
Ann Arbor, Michigan
www.cherrylakepublishing.com

Content Adviser: Dr. Julia L. Hovanec, Professor of Art Education,
Kutztown University, Kutztown, Pennsylvania

Photo Credits: Page 4, ©Petr Jilek/Dreamstime.com; page 6, ©Jahoo/
Dreamstime.com; page 7, ©Pepo971/Dreamstime.com; pages 28 and
30, ©Dana Meachen Rau; page 29, ©Raja Rc/Dreamstime.com; page
32, Tania McNaboe

Library of Congress Cataloging-in-Publication Data
Rau, Dana Meachen, 1971–
Decorating eggs / by Dana Meachen Rau.
p. cm. — (Crafts) (How-to library)
Includes bibliographical references and index.
Audience: Grades K–3.
ISBN 978-1-61080-474-5 (lib. bdg.) —
ISBN 978-1-61080-561-2 (e-book) —
ISBN 978-1-61080-648-0 (pbk.)
1. Egg decoration—Juvenile literature. I. Title.
 TT896.7.R38 2012
745.594'4—dc23   2012006806

Cherry Lake Publishing would like to acknowledge the
work of The Partnership for 21st Century Skills. Please
visit *www.21stcenturyskills.org* for more information.

Printed in the United States of America
Corporate Graphics Inc.
July 2013
CLFA11

A NOTE TO ADULTS:
Please review the instructions for these craft projects before your children make them. Be sure to help them with any crafts you do not think they can safely conduct on their own.

A NOTE TO KIDS:
Be sure to ask an adult for help with these craft activities when you need it. Always put your safety first!

HOW-TO LIBRARY

TABLE OF CONTENTS

Signs of Spring

Fluffy yellow chicks are a common symbol of springtime.

Springtime is filled with many new things. New leaves grow on the trees. New flowers sprout from the ground. Birds lay eggs with new chicks inside. Eggs have become a symbol of spring, and decorating eggs has become a spring holiday tradition.

The signs of spring can be **inspiring**. Go outside and notice the colors and details of the season. Then bring your ideas inside. The hard white surface of an egg makes it a perfect blank space for your design. You can decorate an egg with a rainbow of colors. You can paint an image on the egg's surface. You can draw **abstract** designs.

You can turn a plain white egg into a creative masterpiece.

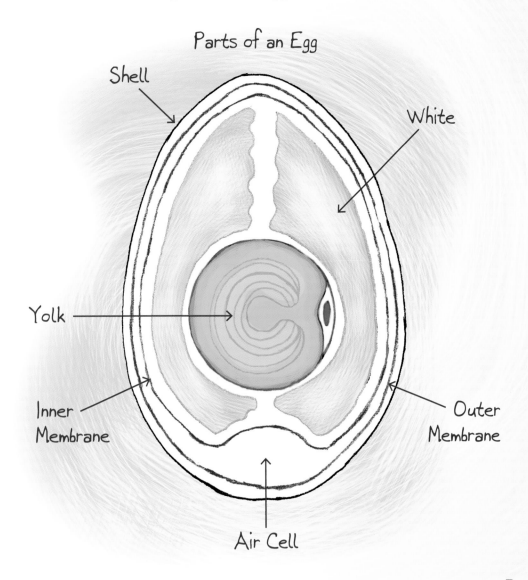

Parts of an Egg

Shell

White

Yolk

Inner Membrane

Outer Membrane

Air Cell

Gifts of Good Wishes

People have decorated eggs for hundreds of years.

For many ancient cultures, eggs symbolized new life. Once the religion of Christianity spread, eggs became an Easter tradition. Christians did not eat eggs during Lent, the time leading up to Easter. People ate eggs when Lent was over, to celebrate the holiday.

Eggs are especially important to people of the Ukraine. Ukrainians have a long folk art tradition called *pysanky*.

Fabergé eggs are very valuable.

Pysanky eggs are decorated with symbols, such as birds, stars, and flowers. People draw on the eggs with wax, then dip them in dye. The dye does not color the waxed parts. Then they warm the wax, wipe it off, and repeat the process to add more areas of color. People take lots of care and time to make pysanky eggs. They give them as gifts to share good wishes. They also believe the eggs protect them from harm and evil.

In the late 1800s, Peter Carl Fabergé brought decorated eggs to a royal level. He worked as the jeweler to the Russian **czars**. He created eggs for them each Easter. But his eggs were not birds' eggs. They were made of gold and gems. His eggs opened to reveal jeweled surprises inside.

Basic Tools

The first thing you need to decorate an egg is an egg, of course! Eggs are sold by the dozen in grocery stores and convenience stores. You can also buy fresh eggs from farmers' markets.

Here are some tools you need to prepare, design, dye, and decorate your eggs:

Preparing eggs

- *Stove, saucepan, and water*—to make hard-boiled eggs
- *Bowl and paper clip or egg blower*—to blow out eggs

Coloring eggs

- *Food dye, vinegar, hot water, and bowls or cups*—for dyeing the eggs
- *Spoons and wire dipping sticks*—for dipping the eggs
- *Empty egg carton and paper towels*—for drying the eggs

Decorating eggs

- *Pencil*—to plan your design and draw on your egg
- *Markers and paint*—to decorate the surface
- *Glitter or stickers*—to add extra flair
- *Glue*—to stick on decorations
- *Electrical tape and rubber bands*—to place on the egg before you dye it, to keep some parts white
- *Water-based varnish*—to help seal your design
- *Wooden skewer and sturdy bottle or tall cup*—to make a stand for a blown-out egg

EGG SIZES
Eggs come in small, medium, large, extra-large, and jumbo sizes. Large eggs are a good size to use for cooking and decorating. Jumbo eggs sometimes have two yolks!

Boiling and Blowing

There are two ways to prepare an egg for decorating—boiling and blowing. Boiling cooks the inside of the egg. You can decorate the shell, then peel it off to eat the white and yolk. If you don't want to see your decoration cracked into little pieces, you can blow out the insides of an uncooked egg and decorate the shell. A blown-out egg can last for years. Ask an adult to help you with these activities.

To Boil an Egg

1. Place the egg in a small saucepan. Fill the pan with water about 1 inch (2.5 centimeters) higher than the egg.
2. Cover the pan and heat it on high. As soon as the water starts to boil, turn the heat off and remove the pan from the burner.
3. Let the pan sit, covered, for about 15 minutes.

STOVE AND FOOD SAFETY
Always be safe. You need the help of an adult when you are working with stoves and boiling water. Both of them can burn you. You need to be safe with food, too. You can only keep hard-boiled eggs out of the refrigerator for up to two hours, and you need to eat them within a week of cooking them.

An egg blower can make it easier to empty your eggshells.

4. Drain off the hot water. Let the egg sit until cooled. If you want to cool it faster, run the egg under cold water.

To Blow Out an Egg

1. Wash the shell of the egg.
2. Straighten out a paper clip. Hold the egg carefully in your hand. Poke a small hole in the top pointy end of the egg with the tip of the paper clip.
3. Flip the egg over. Poke the clip into the broader end of the egg. Carefully crack some shell around the hole to widen it. Then swish the paper clip around inside the egg. This will break up the yolk and the **membranes** around the white.
4. Hold the egg over a bowl. Blow into the egg through the small hole on the top end. The insides of the egg will pour out of the bottom hole. You can also use an egg blower if you don't want to put your mouth on the raw egg. You can buy an egg blower at your local craft store.
5. Fill the egg with water. Hold your fingers over the holes and shake. Blow the water out of the egg. Repeat a few times to completely rinse the inside of the egg.
6. Place the empty shell into an egg carton to drain.

Dye, Dip, and Dry

There are three simple steps to coloring hard-boiled eggs: dyeing, dipping, and drying.

Dyeing

Grocery stores often sell egg-dyeing kits before the spring holidays. But you can color eggs anytime using food dyes from the baking aisle of the grocery store.

Before you start, cover your workspace with newspapers. Wear an apron or smock so you don't get dye on your clothes. Keep a roll of paper towels nearby.

If you buy a kit, follow the directions on the package. Food dyes often come with their own directions for dyeing eggs. In general, you'll need about ¼ teaspoon (1.2 milliliters) of dye, 1 teaspoon (5 ml) of white vinegar, and ½ cup (118 ml) of hot water. The vinegar helps the dye stick to the eggshell.

Don't forget the vinegar!

Be careful not to spill.

Mix these ingredients together in a cup. If your cup is too big, the water won't cover the egg when you put it in. If the cup is too small, the water will overflow when you add your egg. A drinking glass or coffee mug works well.

Dipping

Gently place your egg into the dye with a spoon or a wire dipping stick. Check your egg by lifting it out of the dye. The longer you keep the egg in, the darker its color will get. It's up to you whether you want a **pale** color or a dark color. You can dip blown-out eggs to dye them, too. But it is harder because they float. You'll have to hold the egg under the water.

Drying

Gently lift your egg out of the dye and lay it on a paper towel. **Blot**, don't rub, the egg to dry it. Use an upside-down egg carton as a drying stand. Air will be able to get to the top, sides, and bottom of the egg.

Give your eggs plenty of time to dry.

Designs and Details

Colored eggs look great on their own. It is also fun to decorate them by creating patterns with stripes, spots, and swirls.

Resist Techniques
You can cover parts of the egg to **resist** dye. The parts you cover will stay white. Start with a cool, dry, hard-boiled egg or an uncooked egg that has not been blown out yet.

Crayons
Draw flowers, names, or scribbles on your egg with white crayon. The crayon will resist the dye and stay white.

Rubber Bands
Wrap your egg in rubber bands. After dipping, remove the bands. You'll have interesting stripes left behind.

MAKE A PLAN . . . OR NOT!
Before you start dyeing and decorating, it helps to sketch out designs on paper. Then you'll know what color dyes to mix up and what materials you will need. You don't always need a plan, though. Experiment with colors and ideas as you create your eggs. Interesting patterns might form as you work.

Stickers and Tape

Place stickers or shapes cut from electrical tape on the surface of the egg. Press them down well. After dipping, blot the egg dry and peel off the tape.

Marbleizing

To give your eggs a marbled look, pour your dye mixture into a shallow bowl. Add about a tablespoon (15 ml) of vegetable oil. The oil won't mix with the water—it will form blobs on the surface. Roll the egg around in the dye. Remove, pat it dry, and rub off the oil with a paper towel.

You shouldn't use paint, glue, or markers on eggs that you plan to eat. When eggs are cooked, **bacteria** or other harmful substances can get in through the shell. But you can add sticker decorations or use tape to attach paper cutouts.

Blown-out eggs are made for display, not to be eaten. So you can use any paint, marker, glue, or other material that you would use for any craft project. Use your imagination and treat your egg like an artist's canvas.

Try covering your egg in stars.

Oil can give your egg a fun pattern.

15

Speckled Eggs

If you've ever discovered a nest in a tree, you might have been lucky enough to spot the treasure inside. Nature makes some of the most beautifully decorated eggs. Re-create nests of colorful eggs indoors.

Materials

Blue food dye

Vinegar

Hot water

Cup

Spoon

1 hard-boiled egg

   (*see directions on*

   pages 10–11)

Paper towels

Empty egg carton

Plastic gloves

Paper plate

Old toothbrush

Deep bowl

Steps

1. Mix the blue dye, vinegar, and hot water in a cup with the spoon. (*See pages 12–13 for directions.*)
2. Dip in the egg. Keep it in the dye just long enough to turn it a pale blue color.
3. Remove the egg and pat it dry with paper towels. Set it on the egg carton to dry completely.

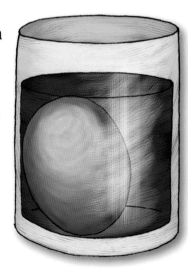

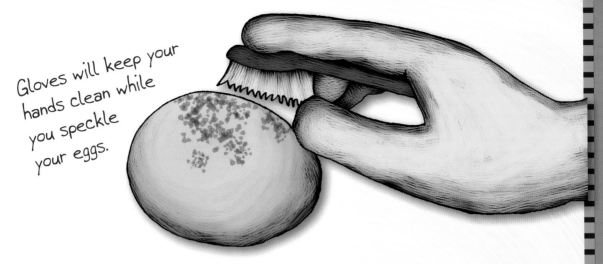

Gloves will keep your hands clean while you speckle your eggs.

4. Put on the plastic gloves. Drip a few dots of blue food dye onto a paper plate.

5. Dip the toothbrush bristles into the dye. Place the egg in a deep bowl. Face the bristles toward the egg. Gently brush your fingers across the bristles so that the dye splatters onto the egg. **Rotate** the egg to cover it all around. The bowl will keep the splatters from getting all over your workspace or your clothes.

6. Set the egg on the egg carton to dry completely. Store it in the refrigerator.

TO DISPLAY YOUR EGG

Cut a grocery bag into lots of thin strips. Scrunch them up with your hands. Place them in a cupcake liner. Place your egg into your paper "nest." You can make a larger nest by filling a grapevine wreath with shredded paper and placing a bunch of eggs on top.

Cut your paper to look like grass or sticks.

Zebra Stripe Eggs

A zebra's stripes help it hide in tall grass. Color an egg with zebra stripes and hide it in its own grassy container.

Materials

Electrical tape
Scissors
1 hard-boiled egg
 (*see directions on
 pages 10–11*)
Green food dye
Vinegar
Hot water
Cup

Spoon
Paper towels
Empty egg carton
Paper towel tube
Green construction paper
Clear tape

Steps

1. Cut the electrical tape into a bunch of **irregular**, long shapes—some pointy, some rounded, and some straight.

Cut your tape into different shapes.

Make sure all of the tape pieces are lying flat.

2. Place the tape pieces all over the egg, pressing well to be sure the pieces are flat.
3. Mix the dye, vinegar, and hot water in a cup with the spoon. (*See pages 12–13 for directions.*)
4. Dip the egg. Keep it in for a while to get a dark color.
5. Pat the egg dry with paper towels. Peel off the electrical tape to reveal white stripes.
6. Set the egg on the egg carton to dry completely. Store it in the refrigerator.
7. With the scissors, cut a 1-inch (2.5 cm) ring from the end of the paper towel tube.

Leave your egg in the dye a little longer than usual.

8. Cut a piece of green construction paper about 6 inches (15 cm) long and 2 inches (5 cm) wide. Cut triangle shapes along the edge of the strip to look like grass.
9. Tape one end of the strip to the paper towel ring. Wrap the strip around and tape the other end closed.
10. Place your egg in the grass holder.

Cut out triangles of different sizes to make your grass look more realistic.

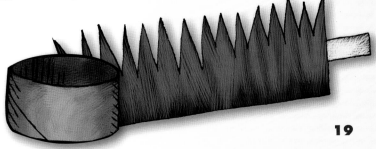

Rainbow Dips

You can create lots of colors from only a few. Red, blue, and yellow are called primary colors. If you mix them together, you can make purple, green, and orange. These are known as secondary colors.

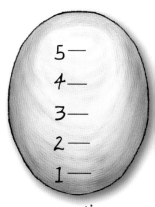

RED + BLUE = PURPLE
BLUE + YELLOW = GREEN
YELLOW + RED = ORANGE

Materials

Pencil
1 hard-boiled egg
   (*see directions on
   pages 10–11*)
Red, blue, and yellow
   food dye

Vinegar
Hot water
3 cups
3 spoons
Wire dipping stick
Paper towels
Empty egg carton

Steps

1. With the pencil, mark five lines evenly across the surface of the egg. Line 1 should be on the pointy end of the egg, and line 5 at the wide end.
2. Mix the red, blue, and yellow dyes with vinegar and hot water in separate cups with the spoons. (*See pages 12–13 for directions.*)

5 —
4 —
3 —
2 —
1 —

Mark your lines
clearly and evenly.

3. With the wire dipping stick (or using your fingers to hold the egg straight), dip the pointy end of the egg into the yellow dye up to the Line 4. Leave it in for just a moment, until it turns a pale yellow color. Remove and pat dry with paper towels.

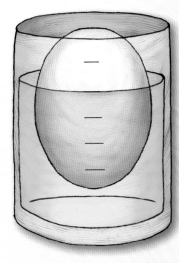

4. Dip the wide end of the egg into the blue dye up to Line 3. Don't leave it in too long. Remove and pat dry. You now have a green stripe where the blue and yellow overlapped.

5. Dip the pointy end into the red dye up to Line 2. Don't leave it in too long. Remove and pat dry. You now have an orange pointy tip.

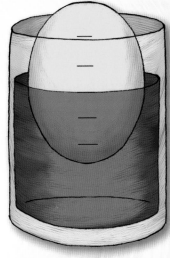

6. Dip the pointy end into the red dye up to Line 1. You can leave the egg in a little longer. You are adding more red to the orange so it turns red. Remove and pat dry.

7. Finally, dip the wide end into the red dye up to Line 5. You can leave the egg in a little longer. You are adding red to the blue to make purple. Remove and pat dry.

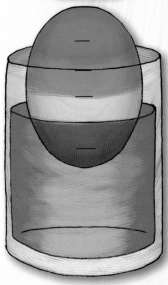

8. Set the egg on the egg carton to dry completely. Store it in the refrigerator.

Stained Glass Eggs

Glue bright splashes of colored tissue paper on this egg. Then fill in the white spaces with black marker to make the design look like a bright stained glass window.

Materials

Wooden skewer
Sturdy bottle or tall cup
Scissors
Colored tissue paper
Water-based varnish
Paper plate
Paintbrush

1 blown-out egg
  (*see directions on
  page 11*)
Tweezers
Black permanent marker

Steps

1. Make a stand for your egg by placing a wooden skewer into the bottle or cup.
2. Cut out small squares and triangles from colored tissue paper.

Don't make your squares too big.

3. Squeeze some varnish onto a paper plate. Dip your paintbrush in the varnish and paint a small area of the egg. Lay a piece of tissue paper on the wet varnish. Then paint over the paper with more varnish.

Use plenty of varnish to make sure the papers stay on your egg.

4. Continue painting small areas of the egg and adding paper shapes. Place them close together with just a little white of the egg showing between them. It's okay if a few of them overlap. Paint over them to keep them in place. If you need to, use tweezers to pick up the paper and place it on the egg.

5. Place the egg on the stand so you can reach all of the sides without having to hold it.

6. When you have covered the egg, paint a thin layer of varnish over the whole surface. Wash your paintbrush before the varnish dries on it.

7. Let your egg dry for a few hours.

8. Color in the white areas with the black marker. If the marker ink does not stick to the egg's surface, let the varnish dry a little longer before trying again.

Make sure the varnish is dry before you color with the marker.

Jeweled Eggs

Treat yourself like royalty. Just like Fabergé, you can create an egg that sparkles like jewelry and display it on a pedestal.

Materials

Glitter
2 paper plates
White glue
1 blown-out egg (*see directions on pages 11*)
Wooden skewer
Sturdy bottle or tall cup
Gold rickrack
Empty spool of thread
Paintbrush

Steps

1. Sprinkle glitter onto a paper plate.
2. Squeeze some glue onto another paper plate or into a disposable container. Use the paintbrush to paint the glue onto a small section of the egg.

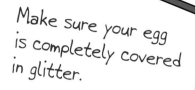

Make sure your egg is completely covered in glitter.

3. Roll the gluey part of the egg onto the glitter.

4. Repeat, painting small areas of glue and rolling the egg in the glitter. As more of the egg gets covered, you can place the egg on a wooden skewer so you don't have to hold it in your hands. Roll it once more in the glitter to make sure it is covered.

5. Place the skewer in the bottle or cup. Let the egg dry for about an hour.

6. Squeeze a ring of glue around the center of the egg and place on the gold rickrack. Let the glue dry.

7. Squeeze glue onto the top of the spool. Place the egg on the pedestal and let it dry.

NATURAL "JEWELS"
Instead of glitter, you can cover an egg with "jewels" such as seeds, dried beans, or sand.

Family Tree Ornament Eggs

A family tree is a way to show how the members of your family are related. Create egg ornaments that look like your parents, siblings, grandparents, aunts, uncles, and cousins.

Materials

Wooden skewer
Sturdy bottle or tall cup
Enough blown-out eggs to
   represent all of your family
   members (*see directions
   on page 11*)
Pencil
Paper plate
Acrylic paint in various colors
Paintbrushes
Fine tip black permanent
   marker

Floral wire
Embroidery floss
White glue

The wooden skewer will keep your egg in place while you work.

Steps

1. Place a wooden skewer into the bottle or cup. Put an egg on this stand.
2. With the pencil, draw a face on the egg to represent a family member.
3. Use the paper plate like a **palette**. Squeeze various colors of acrylic paint on the plate.
4. With a brush, mix colors as needed to get the right skin color.
5. Paint the face of your egg. Set it on the stand. Let it dry for a few minutes.
6. Next, mix up the hair color and paint the hair parts of your egg. Let it dry.
7. Add smaller painted details, such as lips, barrettes, or hair bows. Let the painted egg dry for about an hour.
8. With the marker, draw outlines around each area of color. Use the marker to add small details, too, such as eyes, a nose, earrings, and hair swirls. Add glasses, freckles, or other details that make your family member unique.

Be sure to get the details just right!

9. Repeat, making the other eggs look like the rest of your family.

10. To make your eggs into ornaments, cut a 12-inch (30 cm) piece of floral wire. Fold it in half. Poke it through the bottom hole of the egg and up through the top hole.

11. Cut a piece of embroidery floss about 12 inches (30 cm) long. Thread it through the loop in the top of the wire. Tie the ends of the floss together in an overhand knot.

12. Pull the wire back down through the egg. The knot at the end will keep the floss from coming through the top hole. Remove the wire and tie a knot in the loop end of the floss. You may want to tie it a few times to make sure it is big enough not to slip back through the hole.

13. Pull the string back up through the top hole until it stops at the knot on the loop end. Squeeze a ring of glue around the top to help secure the string.

Be careful not to crack the shell as you pull the wire through.

Eggcellent Ideas

Decorated eggs are fun to make. Invite some friends over for an egg-decorating party. You can provide the dye and some basic craft supplies. Each guest can bring a dozen eggs and a decoration to share.

It is fun to share your eggs when they are done. Make a platter of hard-boiled eggs to serve for the spring holidays. Or turn eggs into ornaments to display for years to come.

Many people decorate eggs to celebrate Easter. But why not make eggs for other holidays, too? You could make heart eggs for Valentine's Day, a clover egg for Saint Patrick's Day, or a flag egg for the Fourth of July. Now that's an eggcellent idea!

Hard-boiled eggs are a tasty treat!

Glossary

abstract (AB-strakt) based on ideas instead of real objects

bacteria (bak-TEER-ee-uh) tiny organisms that can sometimes cause disease

blot (BLAHT) to dry by pressing lightly

czars (ZAHRZ) emperors of Russia

inspiring (in-SPY-ring) able to give you a creative idea

irregular (i-REG-yuh-lur) not standard in shape

membranes (MEHM-braynz) thin skins that line the inside of an egg

pale (PAYL) very light in color

palette (PAL-it) a flat surface for holding and mixing paint

resist (ri-ZIST) to push away from

rotate (ROH-tate) to move around a central point

Another Idea

DECORATING WITH DECOUPAGE
The technique of gluing bits of paper on a surface is called decoupage (day-koo-PAHZH). The varnish creates a seal that holds down the paper and strengthens the egg. You can also cover an egg with cutout words from magazines to make an egg that has something to say!

For More Information

Books

Balchin, Judy. *Decorative Painting*. Chicago: Heinemann Library, 2001.

Barth, Edna. *Lilies, Rabbits, and Painted Eggs: The Story of the Easter Symbols*. New York: Clarion Books, 2001.

Fisher, Diana. *Painting Techniques*. Laguna Hills, CA: Walter Foster, 2005.

Ganeri, Anita. *From Egg to Chicken*. Chicago: Heinemann Library, 2006.

Irvin, Christine M. *Egg Carton Mania*. New York: Children's Press, 2002.

Web Sites

Learn Pysanky

www.learnpysanky.com

Learn more about traditional Ukrainian egg-decorating methods.

Paas Easter Egg Decorating Tips

www.paaseastereggs.com/easter_egg_tips.htm

Check out some tips for preparing and dyeing your eggs.

What's Cooking America: How to Make Natural Easter Egg Dyes

http://whatscookingamerica.net/Eggs/EasterEggDye.htm

Learn how to make your own egg dye from common kitchen items.

Index

About the Author

Dana Meachen Rau is the author of more than 300 books for children on many topics, including science, history, cooking, and crafts. She creates, experiments, researches, and writes from her home office in Burlington, Connecticut.